GIRL ON A MOTORCYCLE

Kenny is going across America by bus to San Francisco. It is a long way, so he stops sometimes and stays the night in a motel.

One evening he stays in a motel in a little town in California – not far from Los Angeles. When he comes down from his room for something to eat, he sees a girl – a girl on a motorcycle, with long blond hair. He thinks he knows her – is she famous?

Then, the next morning, he sees the news about a supermarket robbery in Los Angeles. The police are looking for somebody – somebody on a motorcycle, with long blond hair . . .

OXFORD BOOKWORMS LIBRARY

Crime & Mystery

Girl on a Motorcycle

Starter (250 headwords)

JOHN ESCOTT

Girl on a Motorcycle

Illustrated by
Kevin Hopgood

OXFORD UNIVERSITY PRESS

OXFORD
UNIVERSITY PRESS

Great Clarendon Street, Oxford OX2 6DP

Oxford University Press is a department of the University of Oxford.
It furthers the University's objective of excellence in research, scholarship,
and education by publishing worldwide in

Oxford New York

Auckland Cape Town Dar es Salaam Hong Kong Karachi
Kuala Lumpur Madrid Melbourne Mexico City Nairobi
New Delhi Shanghai Taipei Toronto

With offices in

Argentina Austria Brazil Chile Czech Republic France Greece
Guatemala Hungary Italy Japan Poland Portugal Singapore
South Korea Switzerland Thailand Turkey Ukraine Vietnam

OXFORD and OXFORD ENGLISH are registered trade marks of
Oxford University Press in the UK and in certain other countries

ISBN: 978 0 19 423422 1

A complete recording of this Bookworms edition of
Girl on a Motorcycle is available on audio CD. ISBN 978 0 19 423404 7

Printed in China

Word count (main text): 1300

For more information on the Oxford Bookworms Library, visit
www.oup.com/bookworms

This book is printed on paper from certified and well-managed sources.

CONTENTS

1
Is there a motel?

Kenny is going across America by bus. One evening in summer, his bus arrives in a little town in California.

'I want to stop here tonight,' says Kenny to the bus driver. 'Is there a motel, do you know?'

'Yes,' says the bus driver. 'There's a nice motel across the river. It's not expensive.'

'Is there a bus to San Francisco tomorrow?' asks Kenny.

'Yes,' says the bus driver, 'there's a bus every day.'

Kenny gets off the bus with his bag.

2
Give me the money!

In a street in Los Angeles, somebody is robbing a security guard outside a supermarket. The robber is sitting on a motorcycle and has a gun.

'Give me the money!' the robber tells the security guard.

'OK, OK!' says the security guard, and gives the robber the money.

Then the robber rides away – but a camera is taking pictures.

After the robbery, the supermarket manager phones the police.

'Yes,' he says. 'A robbery . . . yes, long blond hair, and with a motorcycle . . . a man or woman? We don't know . . . yes, we have some pictures . . . OK! Quickly.'

3
Room twenty-three

In the little town, fifty kilometres away from Los Angeles,
Kenny goes into the motel and asks for a room.

'Room twenty-three,' says the man at the desk. He gives
Kenny a key.

'Thank you,' says Kenny. And he goes up to his room.

An hour later, Kenny comes down to eat.

'I'm hungry,' he thinks.

He sees a girl arrive on a motorcycle. She walks to the front desk, and the woman gives her a key.

'Room seventeen,' says the woman at the desk.

'I think I know her face,' thinks Kenny. 'Is she somebody famous?'

4
Is it her?

Early the next morning, Kenny puts on the TV in his room. A news-reader is talking about the supermarket robbery. There are some pictures from the supermarket camera.

Kenny watches the news.

'The robber is somebody with long blond hair, and with a motorcycle,' says the news-reader.

Suddenly, Kenny remembers the girl at the motel desk. 'Is it her?' he thinks. 'Is she the robber?'

5
Can I sit here?

He goes for breakfast. The girl is eating her breakfast at a table near the window. Kenny looks at her. 'Is it her?' he thinks. 'I think I know her, but . . .' He walks across to her table.

'Can I sit here?' he asks.

The girl looks up. 'Well . . . OK,' she says.

Kenny sits down. 'My name's Kenny,' he says.

'Pleased to meet you,' she says. 'I'm Mel.'

'Where are you from?' asks Kenny.

'San Francisco,' says Mel. 'I'm going there later this morning. Where are you from?'

'Boston,' says Kenny. 'I'm going across America by bus. And I'm going to San Francisco later this morning, too.'

'Are you?' the girl says. 'I don't like buses. I like motorcycles. Look, excuse me. I need to make a phone call.'

She gets up and leaves the room.

6
Not the police

A young man near the door is watching Mel.

'Why is he watching her?' thinks Kenny. 'Does he know her face, too? Is *he* thinking she's the girl from the robbery, too?'

Kenny goes to sit next to the young man.

'Hi,' he says. 'My name's Kenny Muir.'

'Hi,' says the young man. 'I'm . . . Ned.'

They begin talking. Kenny tells Ned about the news of the robbery on TV. He looks across at Mel. 'Are you thinking that's the same girl?' he asks Ned.

Ned looks across at her. 'I – I don't know,' he says. 'Perhaps it is.'

'What can we do?' says Kenny. 'She's leaving soon. Let's phone the police. I *think* it's her.'

'No!' Ned says quickly. 'Not the police. Wait . . .'

Kenny looks carefully at him. 'What's the matter? Are you . . . afraid of something?' he asks.

'No, but . . . perhaps she's got a gun!' says Ned.

7
Perhaps I'm wrong

'*Is* it her?' thinks Kenny. 'I want to know. Perhaps the money from the robbery is in her room.'

Kenny goes upstairs. Suddenly he sees the girl again. She is coming out of room seventeen. Kenny watches her. She locks her door and goes downstairs.

'How can I get into her room?' he thinks.

Then Kenny sees a woman working in the motel.

'Excuse me,' says Kenny. 'Can you open the door of my room? My key's in the car. It's room seventeen.'

'Yes, of course,' she says, and opens the door of room seventeen.

'Thank you,' says Kenny, and he goes into the room.

Kenny searches the room, but he cannot find the money from the robbery.

'Perhaps I'm wrong about her,' he thinks.

Then he hears somebody opening the door with a key.

It's Mel!

8
I must get away

Kenny runs into the bathroom. A minute later he hears Mel talking into the phone.

'Hi, Fran,' says Mel. 'No, I'm at the motel . . . No, I'm leaving in an hour . . . Yes, OK . . .'

Kenny looks out carefully from the bathroom. He cannot get to the door, but he can get to the window. He moves quickly.

Mel puts down the phone. Kenny watches her through the window.

'I must get away from here!' he thinks.

Kenny cannot go back into room seventeen, but he can open the window to room eighteen.

9
You're the robber!

Kenny climbs into room eighteen. There is nobody there. He goes across to the door. But then he sees something.

'What's that?' he thinks. 'Is it . . . a *wig*? It is. It's a blond wig!'

Kenny searches the room.

'Here's a black motorcycle coat,' he says to himself. 'And what's this in this bag? The money from the robbery!'

Kenny hears somebody coming. He wants to get out of the room, but he cannot.

Ned comes into the room. He sees Kenny.

'What are you doing in my room?' says Ned.

Then he sees the blond wig and the money. He looks at Kenny again.

'You know!' says Ned.

'Yes, I know!' says Kenny. 'You're the Los Angeles supermarket robber!'

Suddenly, Ned takes a gun from his coat.

'Don't move!' he says. And he takes the bag from Kenny.

'You can't get away,' says Kenny.

'Yes, I can,' says Ned.

He hits Kenny on the head, then he locks him in room eighteen.

10
I can't swim!

A minute later, Mel is looking across at the river from her room. Suddenly, she sees a man running.

'What's the matter with him?' she thinks. 'Why is he running?'

Then she sees Kenny come out of the next room.

'Th – that man!' says Kenny. 'He's the Los Angeles supermarket robber! Stop him, somebody!'

Ned hears him and looks up. Then he gets on his motorcycle and drives off quickly.

'I can stop him!' says Mel.

She climbs down from her room. She runs around the motel, gets on her motorcycle and goes after Ned.

Mel rides her motorcycle quickly towards the river. When she gets to the river, she jumps across the river on the motorcycle, and stops in front of Ned. He cannot stop, and his motorcycle goes into the river.

'Help! Help!' he cries. 'I can't swim!'

11
Can we go slowly, please?

Some people help Ned out of the water. More people are coming from the motel. Kenny runs across to Mel.

'Are you OK?' he asks her.

'Yes, I'm OK,' she says. 'Are you all right?'

'Yes,' says Kenny. 'I'm all right.'

Soon after, the police arrive and take Ned away. Kenny tells a policeman his story. Then Mel tells the policewoman her story.

'Do I know your face?' the policewoman asks Mel. 'Are you famous?'

Mel laughs. 'Perhaps you do,' she says. 'I'm on TV sometimes.'

23

'*Now* I remember you,' Kenny says to Mel. 'You're Mel Palmer, the famous Stunt Girl! I see you on '*Stunt Girls, USA*', on TV sometimes.'

Mel smiles. 'Yes, that's me,' she says. 'Now, do you want to come to San Francisco on my motorcycle, or do you want to go on the bus?'

'I'm coming with you!' says Kenny, laughing. 'But can we go *slowly*, please?'

GLOSSARY

bathroom the room where you can bath and wash

blond a yellow-white colour

climb go up or down using hands and feet

famous a famous person is someone who many people know

gun a thing that shoots bullets to kill people

lock (*v*) use a key in a door

manager someone who controls a business

motel a building where you can pay to stay in a room and
  have your meals

news a TV or radio programme that tells about the things
  that happen

news-reader someone who reads the news

police the men and women who catch criminals

rob take something that is not yours

robber someone who takes something that is not theirs

search look carefully for something

stunt something dangerous and exciting

swim move your body through water using your arms and
  legs

wig false hair

Girl on a Motorcycle

ACTIVITIES

Before Reading

1 **Look at the picture on the cover of the book. Now answer these questions.**

    1 Do you think the story is

        a ☐ funny?

        b ☐ sad?

        c ☐ exciting?

        d ☐ frightening?

    2 Where do you think the story happens?

        a ☐ China

        b ☐ America

        c ☐ England

        d ☐ Italy

2 **Read the back cover of the book. Now answer these questions.**

    1 Do you think Kenny is a policeman?

    2 Do you think the robber shoots Kenny?

    3 Do you think the girl is the robber?

While Reading

1 Read pages 1–4, then answer these questions.

1 How often do buses go to San Francisco?
2 Where is someone robbing a supermarket?
3 The supermarket manager says, 'Yes, we have some pictures.' How does he have pictures of the robber?
4 What is Kenny's room number in the motel?
5 How does the girl in room seventeen arrive at the motel?

2 Read pages 5–8. Now answer these questions.

a) Who

. . . is talking about the robbery on TV?

. . . does Kenny remember who has long blond hair?

b) Where

. . . is the girl eating her breakfast?

. . . are Mel and Kenny going later that morning?

3 Read pages 9–12.
Are these sentences true (T) or false (F)?

	T	F
1 Someone is watching Mel.	☐	☐
2 Ned wants to phone the police.	☐	☐
3 Kenny opens Mel's room with his key.	☐	☐

4 Read pages 13–16. Now answer these questions.

1 Mel comes back to her room. Where does Kenny go first?

2 Who is Mel talking to on the phone?

3 What is the first thing Kenny sees in room eighteen?

4 What is in the bag?

5 Read pages 17–20. Who says or thinks these words?

1 'What are you doing in my room?'

2 'You can't get away.'

3 'Why is he running?'

4 'He's the Los Angeles supermarket robber!'

5 'I can stop him!'

**6 Before you read pages 21–24, can you guess
what happens?**

	YES	NO
1 Ned kills Mel.	☐	☐
2 Mel falls off her motorcycle into the river.	☐	☐
3 Mel stops Ned.	☐	☐
4 Kenny stops Ned.	☐	☐
5 Ned falls into the river.	☐	☐

After Reading

1 Put these twelve sentences in the right order.

a ☐ Kenny sees the girl eating her breakfast.

b ☐ Kenny finds the money from the robbery.

c ☐ Kenny's bus arrives.

d ☐ Ned takes a gun from his coat.

e ☐ Kenny goes into room seventeen.

f ☐ Ned's motorcycle goes into the river.

g ☐ Kenny climbs into room eighteen.

h ☐ Somebody robs a security guard outside
a supermarket.

i ☐ Mel gets on her motorcycle.

j ☐ Kenny hears about the robbery on TV.

k ☐ The police take Ned away.

l ☐ Kenny sees a girl arrive at the motel on a motorcycle.

2 Use these words to join the sentences together.

or but and on

1 Kenny's bus arrives in town. An evening in summer.

2 The robber rides away. A camera is taking pictures.

3 The girl goes to the front desk. The man gives her a key.

4 Do you want to come to San Francisco on my
motorcycle? Do you want to go on the bus?

3 Look at each picture, then answer the questions after it.

1

Who is this?
What is he/she doing?

4

Who is this?
What is he/she doing?

2

Who is it?
What is he doing?

5

Who is riding this
motorcycle?

3

Who is this?
What is he/she doing?

6

Who is writing?

ABOUT THE AUTHOR

John Escott worked in business before becoming a writer. He has written many books for readers of all ages, but enjoys writing crime and mystery thrillers most of all. He was born in Somerset, in the west of England, but now lives in Bournemouth, on the south coast. When he is not working, he likes looking for old books in small back-street bookshops, watching Hollywood films, and walking for miles along empty beaches.

He has written or retold more than twenty stories for the Oxford Bookworms Library. His original stories include *Star Reporter* (Starter, Human Interest), *Goodbye, Mr Hollywood* (Stage 1, Thriller & Adventure), and *Sister Love and Other Crime Stories* (Stage 1, Crime & Mystery).

OXFORD BOOKWORMS LIBRARY

Classics • Crime & Mystery • Factfiles • Fantasy & Horror
Human Interest • Playscripts • Thriller & Adventure
True Stories • World Stories

The OXFORD BOOKWORMS LIBRARY provides enjoyable reading in English, with a wide range of classic and modern fiction, non-fiction, and plays. It includes original and adapted texts in seven carefully graded language stages, which take learners from beginner to advanced level. An overview is given on the next pages.

All Stage 1 titles are available as audio recordings, as well as over eighty other titles from Starter to Stage 6. All Starters and many titles at Stages 1 to 4 are specially recommended for younger learners. Every Bookworm is illustrated, and Starters and Factfiles have full-colour illustrations.

The OXFORD BOOKWORMS LIBRARY also offers extensive support. Each book contains an introduction to the story, notes about the author, a glossary, and activities. Additional resources include tests and worksheets, and answers for these and for the activities in the books. There is advice on running a class library, using audio recordings, and the many ways of using Oxford Bookworms in reading programmes. Resource materials are available on the website <www.oup.com/bookworms>.

The *Oxford Bookworms Collection* is a series for advanced learners. It consists of volumes of short stories by well-known authors, both classic and modern. Texts are not abridged or adapted in any way, but carefully selected to be accessible to the advanced student.

You can find details and a full list of titles in the *Oxford Bookworms Library Catalogue* and *Oxford English Language Teaching Catalogues*, and on the website <www.oup.com/bookworms>.

THE OXFORD BOOKWORMS LIBRARY
GRADING AND SAMPLE EXTRACTS

STARTER • 250 HEADWORDS

present simple – present continuous – imperative –
can/cannot, must – *going to* (future) – simple gerunds …

Her phone is ringing – but where is it?

Sally gets out of bed and looks in her bag. No phone. She looks under the bed. No phone. Then she looks behind the door. There is her phone. Sally picks up her phone and answers it. *Sally's Phone*

STAGE 1 • 400 HEADWORDS

… past simple – coordination with *and, but, or* –
subordination with *before, after, when, because, so* …

I knew him in Persia. He was a famous builder and I worked with him there. For a time I was his friend, but not for long. When he came to Paris, I came after him – I wanted to watch him. He was a very clever, very dangerous man. *The Phantom of the Opera*

STAGE 2 • 700 HEADWORDS

… present perfect – *will* (future) – *(don't) have to, must not, could* –
comparison of adjectives – simple *if* clauses – past continuous –
tag questions – *ask/tell* + infinitive …

While I was writing these words in my diary, I decided what to do. I must try to escape. I shall try to get down the wall outside. The window is high above the ground, but I have to try. I shall take some of the gold with me – if I escape, perhaps it will be helpful later. *Dracula*

... should, may – present perfect continuous – *used to* – past perfect –
causative – relative clauses – indirect statements ...

Of course, it was most important that no one should see
Colin, Mary, or Dickon entering the secret garden. So Colin
gave orders to the gardeners that they must all keep away
from that part of the garden in future. *The Secret Garden*

STAGE 4 • 1400 HEADWORDS

... past perfect continuous – passive (simple forms) –
would conditional clauses – indirect questions –
relatives with *where/when* – gerunds after prepositions/phrases ...

I was glad. Now Hyde could not show his face to the world
again. If he did, every honest man in London would be proud
to report him to the police. *Dr Jekyll and Mr Hyde*

STAGE 5 • 1800 HEADWORDS

... future continuous – future perfect –
passive (modals, continuous forms) –
would have conditional clauses – modals + perfect infinitive ...

If he had spoken Estella's name, I would have hit him. I was so
angry with him, and so depressed about my future, that I could
not eat the breakfast. Instead I went straight to the old house.
Great Expectations

STAGE 6 • 2500 HEADWORDS

... passive (infinitives, gerunds) – advanced modal meanings –
clauses of concession, condition

When I stepped up to the piano, I was confident. It was as if I
knew that the prodigy side of me really did exist. And when I
started to play, I was so caught up in how lovely I looked that
I didn't worry how I would sound. *The Joy Luck Club*

Robin Hood

JOHN ESCOTT

'You're a brave man, but I am afraid for you,' says Lady Marian to Robin of Locksley. She is afraid because Robin does not like Prince John's new taxes and wants to do something for the poor people of Nottingham. When Prince John hears this, Robin is suddenly in danger – great danger.

Star Reporter

JOHN ESCOTT

'There's a new girl in town,' says Joe, and soon Steve is out looking for her. Marietta is easy to find in a small town, but every time he sees her something goes wrong . . . and his day goes from bad to worse.

Goodbye, Mr Hollywood

JOHN ESCOTT

Nick Lortz is sitting outside a café in Whistler, a village in the Canadian mountains, when a stranger comes and sits next to him. She's young, pretty, and has a beautiful smile. Nick is happy to sit and talk with her.

But why does she call Nick 'Mr Hollywood'? Why does she give him a big kiss when she leaves? And who is the man at the next table – the man with short white hair?

Nick learns the answers to these questions three long days later – in a police station on Vancouver Island.

Sister Love and Other Crime Stories

JOHN ESCOTT

Some sisters are good friends, some are not. Sometimes there is more hate in a family than there is love. Karin is beautiful and has lots of men friends, but she can be very unkind to her sister Marcia. Perhaps when they were small, there was love between them, but that was a long time ago.

They say that everybody has one crime in them. Perhaps they only take an umbrella that does not belong to them. Perhaps they steal from a shop, perhaps they get angry and hit someone, perhaps they kill . . .